Book Description

Does your child have a hard time sitting still? Do they have little to no patience when it comes to waiting their turn? Are they always seeking attention using negative behaviors like crying, whining, or throwing temper tantrums? Does their teacher complain of poor focus and attention in class? Are they always interrupting you and others in a hurried manner?

They could have attention deficit hyperactivity disorder (ADHD).

Children with special needs, such as those with ADHD require more love, care, and time. Parents have to be more patient with them as, most of the time, they exhibit behaviors that are out of their control and need to be disciplined. However, that discipline doesn't come in the form of punishment, rather in the form of some helpful, yet effective, parenting rules and skills.

In this brief guide, we review 7 vital parenting skills that have been proven effective when dealing with children who have ADHD. We explore the various means to implement these skills and put them to the test for their effectiveness. We also discuss why parents need to learn and practice these skills. Some of the principal topics discussed include the following:

- Offering children with ADHD structure and its role in behavior modification
- Setting clear expectations to instruct, explain and follow
- Understanding why some mild misbehavior must be ignored
- Introducing the idea of consequences to improve behavior
- Need for positive attention and its impact on children with ADHD
- Learning to block out distractions to improve focus
- Establishing reward systems and knowing their effectiveness etc.

Written to inspire every parent and facilitate them in modifying behavior in their children, this book comes packed with science-backed research and implementable strategies to offer readers some support when dealing with a child with ADHD.

7 Vital Parenting Skills for Teaching Kids With ADHD

Proven ADHD Tips for Dealing With Attention Deficit Disorder and Hyperactive Kids

Frank Dixon

professional advice. The content within this book has been derived from various sources. Please consult a licensed professional before attempting any techniques outlined in this book.

By reading this document, the reader agrees that under no circumstances is the author responsible for any losses, direct or indirect, that are incurred as a result of the use of the information contained within this document, including, but not limited to, errors, omissions, or inaccuracies.

OTHER BOOKS BY FRANK DIXON

How Parents Can Raise Resilient Children:
Preparing Your Child for the Real Tough World of
Adulthood by Instilling Them With Principles of
Love, Self-Discipline, and Independent Thinking

❋ ❋ ❋

How Parents Can Teach Children To Counter
Negative Thoughts: Channelling Your Child's
Negativity, Self-Doubt and Anxiety Into
Resilience, Willpower and Determination

❋ ❋ ❋

The Vital Parenting Skills and Happy Children
Box Set: A 5 Full-Length Parenting Book
Compilation for Raising Happy Kids Who Are
Honest, Respectful and Well-Adjusted

❋ ❋ ❋

The 7 Vital Parenting Skills and Confident Kids
Box Set: A 7 Full-Length Positive Parenting Book
Compilation for Raising Well-Adjusted Children

❋ ❋ ❋

For a complete list, please visit
http://bestparentingbooks.org/books

YOUR FREE GIFT

Before we begin, I have something special waiting for you. Another action-paced book, free of cost. Think of it as my way of saying thank you to you for purchasing this.

Your gift is a special PDF actionable guide titled, ***"Profoundly Positive Parenting: Learn the Top 10 Skills to Raising Extraordinary Kids!"***

As the title suggests, it's a collection of 10 parenting skills that will help you pave the way towards raising amazing and successful children. It's short enough to read quickly, but meaty enough to offer actionable advice that can make impactful changes to the way you parent.

Intrigued, I knew you would be!

Claim your copy of Profoundly Positive Parenting by clicking on the link below and join my mailing list:

http://bestparentingbooks.org/free-gift/

PROFOUNDLY

POSITIVE PARENTING

Learn the Top 10 Parenting Skills
to Raising Extraordinary Kids!

FRANK DIXON

Before we jump in, I'd like to express my gratitude. I know this mustn't be the first book you came across and yet you still decided to give it a read. There are numerous courses and guides you could have picked instead that promise to make you an ideal and well-rounded parent while raising your children to be the best they can be.

But for some reason, mine stood out from the rest and this makes me the happiest person on the planet right now. If you stick with it, I promise this will be a worthwhile read.

In the pages that follow, you're going to learn the best parenting skills so that your child can grow to become the best version of themselves and in doing so experience a meaningful understanding of what it means to be an effective parent.

Notable Quotes About Parenting

"Children Must Be Taught How To Think, Not What To Think."

— Margaret Mead

"It's easier to build strong children than to fix broken men [or women]."

- Frederick Douglass

"Truly great friends are hard to find, difficult to leave, and impossible to forget."

— George Randolf

"Nothing in life is to be feared, it is only to be understood. Now is the time to understand more, so that we may fear less."

— Scientist Marie Curie

Table of Contents

Introduction

Young children are active and impulsive in general. The world is their oyster - they are only discovering more and more every day. That leads to them acting rambunctious, often. When they are joyous, nothing can stop them from climbing the stairs, jumping around the house, and running inside and out. They won't listen when told to sit properly, they fidget and squirm. They prefer going out to explore all that their mind hasn't yet processed, and will cause chaos wherever they go. The point being that it isn't unusual to have hyperactive kids who have trouble remembering things, obeying orders, or listening.

Parents all across the globe go through more or less the same difficulty when raising a child. Sometimes, their kids simply forget to do what they have been told and sometimes, get distracted while doing so. They will drop things, be careless, and get anxious waiting for their turn when playing collaboratively with other children. It is safe to say that this is a normal part of childhood.

The main difference between a child who has ADHD and a child who doesn't is the frequency of these behaviors. A child with ADHD will exhibit these behaviors as the norm, and a child who doesn't might exhibit these behaviors from time to time. The challenges for parents amplify as the symptoms are rather chronic, pervasive, and disruptive. Children with ADHD have trouble at school, have an even harder time making friends and socializing, and need to be reminded of things frequently. The symptoms must be present for at least six months to be diagnosed as a disorder. If diagnosed, it can impair a child's normal development and make it harder for parents to parent them.

Some of the most commonly-associated symptoms and behaviors a child with ADHD exhibits are frustration, becoming easily overwhelmed, trouble regulating emotions, and struggles with cognitive functions. For instance, you may notice some lagging on their part when it comes to tasks such as planning, organizing, staying focused, and remembering details. Their development also takes time to mature. But that doesn't mean that life for them is dull or boring. They can also be some of the most charismatic, popular, and personable people to hang out with.

Caring for a child with ADHD can be draining for both parents. They need extra attention, extra love, and extra explaining for everything they have been told, so you can imagine the amount of time and energy needed to tend to one. Their impulsiveness, chaotic behavior, and fearlessness can make everyday activities such as eating, bathing, or sleeping stressful and exhausting.

But it will be less stressful if you use the 7 vital parenting skills discussed here. To help parents deal with a child with ADHD, our essential parenting skills will come in handy to plan, organize, engage, and improve performance as well as behavior. It will help them teach about discipline, responsibility, and how they can regulate their emotions themselves, giving their parents a little air to breathe.

Let's begin to explore these in detail and learn of ways in which these parenting skills can guide parents.

Chapter 1: Life With an ADHD Child

All kids, especially toddlers, behave out of the norm occasionally. You have run after them to feed them a spoonful of their lunch, and then do the same at dinner. You have ignored their screams as they try to get away with not taking a bath. You have told them to sit tight in the car as you drove down a busy road, but they have ignored the order without a care in the world.

But for some parents, it is much worse. What they have to deal with is constant. This means they don't just have to run after their toddler during meal times but always, just to ensure they don't hurt themselves. They have to repeat their orders several times in a minute to get their child to respond. These instances are so frequent that they begin to hinder the family's ability to lead normal lives. Other children in the house also feel neglected, parents are shamed for having an ill-mannered child and it is difficult to have a peaceful evening out with the family without having everyone staring back in disgust or judgment.

Understanding ADHD

Attention deficit hyperactivity disorder (ADHD) is a chronic condition in the brain which affects a child's ability to control behavior. Unlike other kids, they are unable to process information or stop thinking about something in a jiffy. Children diagnosed with ADHD have trouble controlling their actions and have a hard time mingling and befriending kids their age. They also report trouble getting along with their teachers, siblings, and parents. They have a difficult time learning and grasping new knowledge and have a poor attention span. If there is anything they don't understand or are unable to process, they move onto another thing, without giving it much attention. They are impulsive, which puts them in physical danger. If you are a parent of a child with ADHD, your child may have been labeled as bad or ill-mannered by those who don't know about their condition.

If we look at the statistics, national data reveals that almost 9.4% of children aged 2-17 in the US are living with ADHD. The data also suggests that boys are twice as likely to develop ADHD as compared to their counterparts. The biggest fear most parents have is whether their child will ever be accepted as a normal kid in the world or not. It is natural for them to want to give their kids the best of the best. However, when one kid aces everything and the other lags to grasp even the basics, it can be hard to parent them both at the same time.

To further understand what it looks like to raise a child with ADHD, we must look at the various behaviors they depict and how they differ from those demonstrated by another child without ADHD. These behaviors are divided into three categories – inattention, hyperactivity, and impulsivity.

A child with inattention behaves in the following manner:

- Daydreams
- Doesn't listen
- Gets distracted easily
- Doesn't follow through the instructions given to finish a task
- Makes careless mistakes
- Doesn't care about the details or steps of things
- Forgetfulness
- Poor organizational skills
- Misplaces or loses items
- Avoids doing things requiring mental effort frequently

A child with hyperactivity behaves in the following manner:

- Is always moving around as if driven by a battery
- Has trouble staying seated
- Talks too much
- Fidgets and squirms
- Can't play in peace and makes noises

A child with impulsivity behaves in the following manner:

- Speaks and acts without thinking
- Running around without an awareness of their surroundings
- Has trouble waiting for their turn

- Doesn't like to share

Although the exact cause of ADHD is still under scrutiny, research suggests that it is due to neurological and biological factors. Some risk factors, however, put your baby at risk of developing the disorder. These include the following:

Biological: It can be caused by biological factors when there is a chemical imbalance in the way neurotransmitters function. Neurotransmitters regulate behavior. An imbalance may cause a child to develop ADHD before or after birth.

Hereditary: Your baby is also at a higher risk of developing ADHD if one or both the parents are diagnosed with ADHD.

Prenatal exposure: Although there isn't any direct link or evidence to prove this, smoking and drug abuse during pregnancy can also be linked with ADHD in children.

Environment: If the child has been exposed to poisons or harmful toxins in the environment such as exposure to lead, they may also exhibit signs of ADHD.

Common Challenges With a Child With ADHD

According to research published in the Journal Pediatrics, 70% of diagnosed children with ADHD suffer from at least one other physical or mental problem such as anxiety, learning disability, depression, and speech or hearing disability (Law et al., 2014). Also, one in five of these kids with ADHD have more than three or more mental or physical problems, increasing their chances of lagging behind in school and professional life.

Parents who are raising a child with ADHD along with others, experience enormous stress and struggle to cope with the symptoms while being stigmatized by their friends, family, and community. Even they experience burdensome emotions and resort to social distancing and isolation from gatherings to feel normal. Before we move onto revealing the 7 vital parenting skills that help parents cope with the symptoms associated with ADHD in their child, we must look at the challenges they have to face being a parent.

One study suggests that approximately 23% of married couples raising a child with ADHD under eight years of age get divorced as opposed to nearly 12% without an ADHD child (Wymbs et al., 2008). It is easy to imagine how this must look for couples who are unable to spend time by themselves as a couple and bond because they have to attend to their child with ADHD constantly.

Boredom is another common, yet neglected, drawback of living with an ADHD child. As they need to be tended to 24/7, and need instructions to be repeated often, it leaves parents with little time to do the things that interest them or that they enjoy. Due to a low attention span, the child also needs regular doses of entertainment to stay engaged, which means that parents have to come up with new and interesting things to keep them engrossed in one thing. Consistency and the need to repeat instructions can also become monotonous and tiring.

Isolation is another challenge that parents have to deal with, especially when they are a single parent and raising a child with a learning or attention deficit disorder. It becomes hard to raise them with empathy and love. When they feel constantly criticized by others for their poor effort to have a hold on their child, they start to feel like they are the only ones going through it, and begin to feel hopeless about the situation getting any better in the future.

And finally, they feel guilt. They think that it is somehow their fault that they gave birth to a child with ADHD. They also feel depressed when they notice that their other kids are being neglected of the attention and love that they deserve. They blame themselves when they are out of control. They blame themselves for not doing enough to keep them calm and help them get better. They feel disheartened when they see them miss out on all the wonderful experiences kids their age generally have.

Nonetheless, here's the thing. There is not much they could have done to prevent it. It isn't their fault and whatever they are doing, the many hours they are putting in and the extra love and affection they are bestowing on them is commendable. However, they can modify things a little bit and develop skills to deal with your unique circumstance better. The changes required aren't much and just offer a new perspective to view things differently and stop feeling helpless and depressed and be prepared to give them the best life and future possibilities.

Chapter 2: The 7 Vital Parenting Skills to Deal With an ADHD Child

It isn't a secret that children diagnosed with ADHD need extra attention, time, and love. We want to see them as successful as our other children or as their peers. We fear that if we don't do enough, they might lag behind and never be able to achieve success.

This isn't true. Did you know some of the most successful people of their time have this neurological disorder? For example, Michael Phelps, the international Olympic swimming champion, battled with ADHD during childhood and a significant part of his adolescence (Celebrity Spotlight: How Michael Phelps' ADHD Helped Him Make Olympic History, n.d.). Recipient of 28 gold medals and one of the most successful and celebrated American heroes, he had a difficult time in school and was known to act out and disrupt the class. It was in the pool that he found some calm and relaxation which allowed him to let this mind and body stay on track and focused. He once had a teacher in his class who told him that his misbehavior will ruin his adult life and he will never amount to anything significant.

Another well-known individual, parenting more than 400 companies under the name Virgin Group, Sir Richard Branson also dealt with ADHD during his childhood. Richard, as recalled by his teachers and peers, was always erratic and a misfit (LaMagna, 2018). Richard himself wrote that school was the most dreadful time in his life as he had no understanding of what was being taught. Today, the world knows him as one of the smartest business magnates and investors.

If we look at some celebrities, we come across big names like Jim Carrey, Adam Levine, Paris Hilton, Channing Tatum, Howie Mandel, and Justin Bieber, who have all struggled with attention deficit or hyperactivity disorder.

Although their success is their own doing, a major behind-the-screen role is played by the family, especially their parents. They are the ones who raise them, encourage them to dream big, help them navigate through their dreams and passions, and watch them with pride in their eyes as they soar higher and higher.

When raising a child with special needs, parents are expected to do more. They are expected to stand up for their kids, protect them from the world, and raise them as confident, resilient, and self-reliant adults.

To do so, you need the right resources and rules to live by.

To get you started on the right foot, we are now going to reveal the 7 vital parenting skills to understand, help, and raise children with ADHD. The 7 parenting skills aren't just tools for you but also for your child to learn from so that when they grow up, they learn to manage their behavior themselves effectively.

The 7 Vital Parenting Skills for Teaching Children With ADHD

Parenting Skill #1: Provide Structure

Structure and routines are an essential part of raising a child with ADHD. Structures and set routines have proven to be helpful in minimizing negative or hyperactive behaviors, thanks to their predictability.

Parenting Skills #2: Set Clear Expectations

Clear expectations from the start is another smart way to discipline children with ADHD. It helps them comprehend what is expected of them and what tasks and chores they need to perform. This eliminates confusion and frustration.

Parenting Skill #3: Establish Reward Systems and Praises

The reason rewards and recognition work wonders for children with ADHD is because it keeps them motivated and driven. Rewards, when they come in the form of privileges, can be appealing and even limit misbehavior.

Parenting Skill #4: Eliminate Distractions

Distractions are our biggest enemies and it is only more threatening and scary for a child with ADHD. They seem so tempting that the child is unable to hold back, and gives in to its instant gratification. Thus, we must keep distractions at bay and help children not fall prey to them.

Parenting Skill #5: Set Reasonable

Consequences

Reasonable consequences, like expectations, also work in the same manner. When kids know which behaviors will be rewarded and which will lead to punishments, they are in a better state of mind to modify their behaviors. Thus, as parents, we have to let them know the consequences of their actions beforehand so that they abstain from them.

Parenting Skill #6: Ignore Mild Misbehavior

Most of the time, children with ADHD act out of character to seek attention from their parents. They want parents to stay engaged with them constantly, and when they don't, they often resort to negative behaviors so that the parent has to attend to them. This can make a parent mad and stressed out. However, instead of letting them win and gaining that attention, as parents, we have to choose our battles wisely. We have to learn to ignore some misbehavior so that they aren't encouraged and repeated.

Parenting Skill #7: Give Positive Attention

Positive attention improves interactions. When children with ADHD feel valued and cared for, they are more likely to behave and curb bad behaviors. Receiving positive attention from parents, whether in the form of rewards, quality time, or praises can encourage them to abide by the rules set by the parents and learn to regulate their emotions efficiently.

Chapter 3: Vital Parenting Skill – Provide Structure

If you have a child with ADHD, it mustn't be the first time you hear people tell you that to make your life a whole lot easier, you need to have some structure in your child's life. This comes up as the first piece of advice given by child specialists and healthcare professionals because its effectiveness is, indeed, a life-saver. A structured environment in the house, and routines they can follow-through with easily makes them more efficient and easy to handle. But what does it mean to have structure in life and why is it so important for them?

Being the first vital parenting skill, we are going to explore the idea of what it means to offer children with ADHD a structured environment, how it helps them and how we can create one.

In the simplest of terms, a structured environment is one where there is predictability and organization. The day-to-day routines and tasks are defined in details that are simple to pick up and easy to follow. It involves consistently doing the same things without any unpredicted changes in the sequence or transition. For instance, if your child is expected to have breakfast first and then get dressed, you can't change it without prior notice as it may cause chaos. Similarly, expectations must also be clear from the start (more on this in the next chapter), and the child must also be clear about the consequences of their actions. When these conditions are met, it allows for a predictable and structured environment to be created.

In structured environments, kids are aware of the expectations others have of them. They know what they need to do to finish a task. This further creates a sense of security.

The Importance of Routines and Structure

Children need routines and structure because they are unable to control their impulses otherwise. They have a hard time regulating themselves and their behaviors. With structure comes predictability and focus. When things follow an order, it is difficult to get off track and thus, helps with the elimination of distractions.

With properly enforced routines, children with ADHD can set aside a chunk of time for something, say their homework, every day with consistency. It also helps them get a sense of "what's to come next." For example, if they have the habit of taking out their school clothes, polishing their shoes, and organizing their school bag the night before school, it makes them ready for the next morning. This also sets a clear explanation of what will happen the next morning and make it less chaotic.

Routines in the life of an ADHD child helps them in two ways. First, it improves their daily functioning and efficiency. Their impulsive behavior also remains under control and things start to become manageable.

Second, it eases off some pressure from the parents and other family members as they benefit from it psychologically too. You can expect less drama and decreased stress during family times such as when eating out or doing something together at home, such as watching a movie or doing homework. This leads to a relaxed environment for everyone in the house and helps strengthen the bond in the family.

How to Implement Structure in an ADHD Child's Life

In times when our routines are getting more hectic, it becomes impossible to provide our children with a structured routine. Work keeps us occupied even during off-hours, social media browsing has become a requisite we can't escape from, and competition is only increasing day by day, demanding that we do more and more for our kids to ensure they are raised with the best values and skills possible. You drop your kids off to school, rush to work, then pick them up from school during lunch hour and then drop them off to their practice and then go home, cook, clean, and spend time with your children, and help them with their homework.. So how can you possibly set a routine to be followed? Well, that is debatable, but here's the thing: if you do offer them structure and routine, it will improve their productivity, mental health, and family relationships as well as make them feel confident.

To help you get started, we have created a basic schedule for what a day should look like for a child with ADHD. Keep in mind, not all activities are to be incorporated in the checklist you draft for your child. However, the more elaborative and simple-to-read it is, the better.

Starting with the morning routine, it should look something like this:

Waking up: Stick with the same wake-up time to make mornings easier, every day. If your child is old enough to understand the concept of an alarm clock or timer, they can set one for themselves. If your kid is a toddler or below the age of five, you can wake them up gently with singing or calling their name.

Bathroom routine: This can come in the form of a checklist that contains tasks like taking a shower, using the loo, brushing their teeth, brushing their hair, and putting on school clothes. You can have these written on a piece of paper and stick it on the door of the washroom as a friendly reminder.

Breakfast: They should be offered no more than two options for breakfast, as more choices can be confusing and time-consuming to pick from. Ensure that you cook something nutritious and healthy to make them feel energized. If they are expected to take their medicine, make sure to keep it on the table within their reach to remind them to take it.

Additional chores: If it is the weekend and the child has no school, you can create a list of chores you expect them to finish before lunchtime. It can involve helping you with laundry, doing their homework, cleaning their room or going grocery shopping. Ensure that all these tasks are planned and agreed upon a day before so that they don't come as a surprise. If some tasks involve more than one step that needs to be done in a specific order, then make sure that it is communicated before they start.

An after school routine should look something like this:

Cleaning up: If they have just returned from school, have a list of things they need to do before they come to the table for lunch. This can include changing into clean clothes, washing their hands and face, placing their bag, dirty clothes, shoes, and water bottle in its place.

Homework time: Once they are up or done playing, they must take out their books and study material, and start studying or completing their homework. You can plan a few breaks in between like a fifteen minutes break time after studying for forty-five minutes.

Relaxation or playtime: Set some time aside for unstructured play every day after they are done with their homework. It is up to them to utilize that time. They can watch TV, play board games or with their toys (if they are young).

Clean-Up: Once they are done playing, take out half an hour to clean-up. If they played with their toys in their room, tell them to put them in the basket and clean their room before coming to the dinner table.

The bedtime routine should look something like this:

Getting ready for bed: Again, this should comprise several tasks to be completed before getting into bed. This can mean washing their face, brushing their teeth, changing into pyjamas, etc.

Prepping for tomorrow: They should also pick out the outfit for the next day, organize their school bag, set their dress, help their parents pack lunch, and organize any clips or accessories

Sleeping time: Many children with ADHD have trouble sleeping. A ten minute massage or back rub, as well as reading a short story before tucking them in bed and kissing them good night can help calm them down.

This is just a guide of what a day in the life of a child with ADHD can look like. You can always add or subtract activities and chores based on their age, the intensity of hyperactivity, or inattention.

Chapter 4: Vital Parenting Skill - Set Clear Expectations

The second most important parenting skill that parents today must become pros at is setting clearly-defined, step-by-step, and well-guided expectations. Kids, in general, need to know what is expected of them. They need to know what others expect of them in terms of respect, empathy, and discipline. They need to know what behaviors to model in different settings such as when going to a playground versus a library. They need to know how they must present and carry themselves.

Expectations also serve as a motivating force. When expectations are high and promise great rewards, children give their best shot and try to do better. They excel when they know that what is expected of them is reasonable and attainable. However, when expectations aren't realistic, such as expecting a child to do math problems at a sixth grade level when they are only in the third grade, they will get discouraged. Expectations must be achievable. Sure, they should push children to give their best, but shouldn't be too high, or they will end up feeling like a loser when they fail to live up to unrealistic expectations.

When setting expectations for ADHD children, parents need to be a little more patient and elaborate. They can't just write something on a piece of paper and expect their child to follow it. No, they need to lay out, in clear terms, what is expected and in what capacity, what resources are to be used, and what know-how they will need to accomplish the task. Only then, can the desired outcome be achieved.

The best way to communicate expectations is via rules and routines. When creating rules and routines for kids with ADHD, parents and teachers need to account for the developmental delay and lagging in cognitive functioning skills. They need to treat them as special and offer extra support, encouragement, and details. The goal should be to accommodate the challenges they face and help them polish their skills and talents to be able to achieve success.

This all begins with breaking the tasks into smaller bite-size chunks that are easy to understand, process, and follow.

Importance of Breaking Tasks Into Digestible Chunks

The benefits for breaking tasks into sizable chunks, are various. For starters, kids with ADHD have a hard time concentrating or staying engaged in a single activity. So when things are broken into smaller tasks, it becomes easier for them to focus and stay attentive and engrossed. This makes the accomplishment of tasks easier and more manageable for parents. This trick isn't only applicable to children with disorders or disabilities.

It applies equally to kids and adults, both without any disabilities, as it prevents another critical problem i.e. distractions. With a short attention span, as little as three seconds, children with ADHD have a hard time staying put both physically and mentally. One can't do much about the wandering of thoughts which hinders task or chore completion or at least, impairs its efficiency. But when tasks are broken into digestible and clear sub-tasks, they become easier to handle and the fear of becoming distracted goes away.

Not to mention, clear instructions and step-by-step guidelines allow children with ADHD to accomplish things that they would never otherwise. Be it wearing the right shoe on the right foot or putting their toys back in the toy basket, everything becomes possible when parents give them the knowledge that they need in a way that is easy to understand.

Finally, when tasks are laid out in stages and expected to be completed in a sequence, they become doable, which results in a boost in their confidence. Everyone, not just kids, feels accomplished and motivated to take on another bigger challenge when they accomplish something they didn't think they could. They feel confident in their abilities and proud of themselves to have made it this far. They are more willing to step out of their comfort zones and do more than what they initially thought of doing. The same happens for children with ADHD. When they complete a task successfully, they feel more driven and confident. They want to experience the happiness and peace that comes with their achievement more often, and thus are more determined to behave and carry themselves better. Therefore, you can expect this breakdown to help them gain more confidence in their abilities, as well as boost their self-esteem which leads to increased happiness and satisfaction – things they desperately crave.

How to Do It?

When the aim is to set clear expectations, there are many essential things you need to do first. For instance, you have to ensure that while you are briefing them about your expectations, you have their full attention. This calls for the elimination of any distractions that may make their mind wander. Second, you have to be strategic with the way you instruct them. You can't expect them to follow chain commands where you direct them to complete several tasks in one sentence and believe that they will remember all of them to a tee. For example, you can't tell them, "Get dressed, comb your hair, brush your teeth, and then come downstairs to put on your coat and shoes before getting in the car." They are bound to forget a few of your instructions, as the developmental delay and slow cognitive functioning will make it difficult for them to follow through all the commands. Therefore, you have to make them simple, understandable, and singular. You can ask them to get dressed and wait until they complete that task, before ordering them the second thing. Other than that, you can:

Make a Chores List

A chores list is a form of a to-do list used by professionals and adults to mark important events, tasks, and assignments. To make expectations more clear and comprehensible, you can write them on a piece of paper and stick it in a place with maximum exposure. If you expect them to complete their homework first before playing, have it documented so that they know what is expected of them at all times.

Watch Out for Good Behavior

The reason you need to do so is so that you can praise them the minute it happens. Being praised feels good and happiness is only multiplied when a child with ADHD experiences it. Therefore, always look out for the behaviors they do well and appreciate them for it. This will increase the likelihood of those behaviors being repeated and transformed into a habit later on.

Show Empathy

For parents, listening to their child with ADHD with empathy and compassion is another excellent way to promote communication and strengthen the bond. The more communicative you two are, the more likely you will be able to discipline them. Children with ADHD are often belittled for being different than other kids their age. When they fail to do well in school like their peers, they feel demotivated. They start to think that there is something wrong with them and thus, may become depressed or anxious. If you lend a compassionate ear to listen to them and empathize with them to make them feel normal again, it can help manage their behavior. Listening with empathy also opens the door for collaborative problem-solving and skills development whilst ending in many teachable moments.

Provide Redirection

Sometimes, despite having been told repeatedly what is expected of them, they forget or become distracted. If such is the case with your little one too, redirection and gentle reminders are a great way to get them back on track and complete the tasks at hand. They may need some more explanation and time, but they will eventually finish it.

Set Timers

Another way of keeping track of the time required for a task is by using timers to keep them focused and attentive. When they know that time is running out, they are more likely to stick to the task and not procrastinate or get distracted.

Chapter 5: Vital Parenting Skill – Establish Reward Systems and Praise

Whatever the goal, appreciation, praise, and rewards can be highly uplifting and motivating, not just for children with an attention or focus problem, but for everyone. Whenever we try to achieve something or take up a new goal, it is the rewards and the result that serves as the motivation to keep going. Take getting slim for instance. When you are trying to lose weight, what is it that drives you to the gym every day or makes you jog for several miles? The fact that you will lose weight, and feel good about yourself. The image you have in your mind of a slimmer you is what drives you to keep pushing and doing another lap.

Even our pets seem to take note of this. When they know they will be rewarded with their favorite treats, they behave well. So how can our little ones be any different? Besides, they have always wanted to impress us and when we reward their effort, it just fills their heart with joy and a sense of pride. They feel confident in themselves and in their abilities, making them more likely to aim for more challenging things.

Since the goal with ADHD children is mostly behavior improvement, a reward system and frequent praise can help a lot. It can be the difference between positive and negative behavior. To them, recognition for a job well done means more than what it means for kids without an attention and hyperactivity-related disorder.

The Role of Positive Praise and Appreciation

But do positive incentives work? According to one research study published in the journal Biological Psychiatry, it does!

Researchers from Nottingham University conducted a series of experiments on children with ADHD to know how and if they benefit from immediate rewards in the same way as they do when giving the medicine Ritalin (Groom et al., 2009). Ritalin is a behavior modification medication prescribed to children and adults with ADHD to control their behavior and tone down the hyper-activeness a little.

During the study, researchers aimed to examine how rewarding children for good behavior impacted their brain's functioning. The children that participated were asked to play a computer video game devised by the researchers. Their brain's functioning was monitored via electroencephalogram (EEG). The biggest challenge in the game was to catch aliens of a certain color. The results proved that receiving immediate rewards did improve their performance in almost the same manner as did the Ritalin –although to a lesser degree. But when the researchers amplified the rewards as well as the punishments in the game – the children's brains showed signs of complete normalcy.

Hence, they were able to deduce that incorporating reward systems in the lives of children with attention and hyperactivity disorder can result in performance improvement as well as behavior modification. This is hopeful for parents who want to avoid medication, as it means that our children won't have to rely only on traditional medication like Ritalin and engage in alternative programs to stabilize their behavior in the longer run. This possibility is indeed a rewarding one and can help parents as well as teachers all around the world to guide children with ADHD like other 'normal' children.

5 Ways to Make Your Child With ADHD Special

Now that we know that medication and praise can have the same impact on behavior and help improve it, how can we incorporate reward systems in their daily lives to enhance productivity and build focus? The first step is to eliminate problem behaviors. Meaning, we need to know which behaviors we need to reward and which ones to eliminate. Yes, you have to reward them for things that they aren't doing as well, such as not yelling or shouting their answers in the class and holding up their hands patiently. When we classify positive and negative behaviors in this manner, we will be able to improve interactions in a more suitable manner.

Introduce a Token Economy System

What is a token economy system? If we look at its literal definition, it goes something like this: a token economy is a form of behavior modification where the goal is to increase desirable behavior and limit or decrease undesirable ones (Morin, 2019). The children receive tokens for every positive action and behavior. They collect these and then exchange them for something of higher privilege. This also encourages them to learn patience as they delay the final dose of gratification throughout the day. To start with this, you can simply use coins or sheets of paper in different colors, cut into circles like a badge. You can also substitute it for stickers in the shape of a star. Next, you have to create a list of chores or tasks that you want them to perform throughout the day, like helping fold the laundry, taking a bath, organizing their room, putting their toys back, completing their homework, etc. Once they complete those actions, you give them a circle or place a star in front of the completed task. Now comes the step where you set up the rewards. They can range from simple things like getting an hour of free time to things like getting ice-cream after dinner. The more tokens they collect, the bigger the reward.

Praise the Effort, Not the Output

Praise, whether it comes in the form of a tangible or intangible reward, can build their self-esteem. As their parent, it is your job to appreciate them for their effort, regardless of whatever the outcome is. If you know that they put all their heart into something, it doesn't matter if they win or not. What matters is their concentration, focus, and effort to try to win. That, in itself, is something to boast about.

Be Specific With Praises

Be elaborative and specific so that they know what they are being praised for specifically. For example, if you notice that they help you set the dinner table without being asked, let them know that you appreciate them by specifically pointing out that action. Instead of saying, "Thank you, I appreciate it," say something like, "I am so glad you helped me with setting the table. I am very grateful. You are such a good kid." The latter seems to offer more recognition for a particular action. Chances are, they will start doing it more often, just for the sake of being praised and recognized.

Offer Immediate Feedback

Unlike most kids, children with ADHD need constant motivation and supervision. One of the most effective ways to help them stay focused is through immediate feedback. This means that if they are doing something, and that task involves several steps, you have to encourage them at each step and offer positive feedback on how well they are doing so that they stay attentive and motivated.

Frame Praises Positively

Saying something like, "Thank you for not shouting," or, "Thank you for staying put in the car," aim to make your praises more positive and uplifting. You can also say things like, "I am so proud of you for staying calm," or, "I feel so happy that you have behaved so well in the car." This will automatically point out the actions you are encouraging and praising and not the actions that you are trying to diminish.

Chapter 6: Vital Parenting Skill – Eliminate Distractions

The very definition of distractibility means that an individual is unable to block out unimportant distractions, both mental and visual, and stay focused on the important matter at hand. Even for us, it can be hard to focus on things at times. Take a boring and slow day in the office, for instance. Nothing exciting comes up and you have been looking at spreadsheets all day. You will crave distractions if they aren't already present. Even the little crack in the wall will seem more interesting than doing the actual work. What you are doing is deliberately trying to distract yourself and avoid doing something important.

However, the only difference between you and a child with ADHD is that they don't have to deliberately distract themselves. Even the slightest of noises such as whispers in the classroom or a visual distraction like a bird sitting on a branch of a tree in the garden distracts them. They are unable to control their impulses and prevent themselves from being distracted and procrastinating. They will be distracted if their pet walks by or a cabinet in the kitchen is opened by you and have a hard time going back to doing what they were doing. Sometimes, distractions are so intense and serious that they forget about what they were doing beforehand. For example, you may have asked your kid to get a book from their bag from their room that is upstairs. They may have started the journey towards the stairs with a focused mind but ended up being distracted by the toy basket in their room. While you wait for them to get back, they may have already started on a puzzle.

Simply put, children with ADHD lack the filters other kids have to block out any distractions in the environment.

Why Distractions Are Your Biggest Enemy

A child with ADHD may not respond well when trying to listen or pay attention to something. They are more likely to start daydreaming, focus on other things of interest, look out the window or pay attention to noises like the chirping of the bird, the sound of the wind, and the movement of the leaves on a tree. When this happens, they are unable to stay in the moment. They are unable to pay attention to what is happening in the present or follow directions, lessons, or instructions. As we now know, ADHD isn't a disorder where the individual is unable to pay attention, it is about being unable to control attention. This is due to the low level of brain arousal which makes screening out of distractions in the external environment almost impossible. This means they can't be blamed or punished for being inattentive because it isn't their doing – it is how their brain functions.

When a child with ADHD becomes distracted, they require more time than others to finish a task or chore. They also need more convincing and encouragement than most kids to stay focused and not let their minds wander off. This causes delays. Similarly, if we evaluate their performance at school, they require more time to grasp new information and not miss out on some due to distractions. They need to make more efforts to learn, process, and retain information.

Strategies to Prevent the Distraction Trap

Have you ever noticed how your child can focus intently on a few things but not all? Like, if they are playing a video game on the computer or looking out of the car as you drive past restaurants, they can maintain focus and recall the scenes frame-by-frame when questioned. But when it comes to other activities like doing their homework, staying attentive in the classroom, or doing some other chore, they fail to achieve that level of focus and concentration. Ever wondered why that is?

Hyper-focusing is an experience where one can achieve intense bouts of focus and concentration, something common with people with ADHD. To be more specific, ADHD doesn't always mean that the child or adult has an attention deficit. Sometimes, it is the inability to regulate the attention span to the desired task (Flippin, 2007). Thus, during some mundane tasks, it is hard to stay focused unlike on others that are completely absorbing.

So how can you increase your chances of improving their focus and eliminating distractions? We have listed below some of the best strategies to choose from.

Maintain Eye Contact

It is very hard to keep your mind from straying when you suffer from a disorder like ADHD. This means conversations are a nightmare for some as they are easily distracted and lose track of what's being said, and hurt the feelings of the speaker. It can also lead to an argument. For example, you are in the middle of scolding your teenager with ADHD for being so careless about their hygiene and you notice that they are in another world, daydreaming about something else. Would that not make you madder than before? But it is rarely in their control. However, to keep matters from getting worse, encourage that they maintain eye contact with you, and you with them. This can help them stay in the moment and remain attentive.

Give Medication on Time

Medications are not only a necessity to improve behavior but also a life-saver when trying to build focus and concentration. Ensure that your child is taking their medication on time and regularly.

Introduce Active Learning

Active learning involves the usage of external tools, such as colored pencils, highlighters, stickers, and other artistic or creative things to encourage learning. For instance, if your child is doing math homework, you can make use of their marbles to help them get the right answers. Similarly, if there is something you want to highlight in their textbook or say, on a chores list, you can always underline it, write it using colored pencils or make it bold to be easily spottable. This will help build and maintain both focus and interest.

Let Them Catch a Breath

Short breaks during work can help too. It allows the child's brain to relax for a while and then get back to work while being in a more refreshed state. This also prevents things from becoming tedious and makes the workload manageable.

Break Up Tasks Into Shorter Sub-Tasks

Sometimes, a task seems uninteresting because it is too lengthy or time-consuming. However, if we strategically divide it into smaller sections and treat each section as an individual task, it will become more interesting and doable. Using this trick with your child with ADHD can also prove helpful when the goal is to eliminate distractions and improve focus. You can also add a ten-minute break time between each task to let their mind take a break and then get back to work. Besides, the act of ticking off each separate task will serve as motivation for the next one and keep your little one engaged and attentive. This will also minimize the overall amount of time spent on the task and improve efficiency.

Encourage Self-Monitoring

If the child is old enough to take care of themselves, it is best to teach them to self-monitor and identify the triggers that distract them. With some practice and time, they will be able to spot the triggers and become aware of them and what damage they cause. Thus, the minute they feel like drifting off, they will seek help or engage in self-talk to get back to work.

Supervise

If they are unable to self-monitor, you can supervise and help them stay focused. You can always start by giving them a distraction-free space in the house. If that isn't possible, you can sit with them while they take on some activity or try to do their homework to keep their mind from wandering off. You can repeatedly talk them into getting back to their work. Over time, the strict supervision can turn into frequent check-ins where you leave them on their own, with perhaps a designated time, to finish a task and check up on them often to see if they are still focused or not.

Chapter 7: Vital Parenting Skill – Set Reasonable Consequences

We all have been told from time to time that failure is the best teacher. How many times have we allowed them to fall or get hurt so that they would learn the lesson? There have been instances when knowing the solution to their problems, we have taken a step back and let them figure it out on their own. We have seen them making a bad decision or a poor choice and yet not done anything to stop it. But letting them make poor decisions should also come with a price. If you are letting them fail, you have to let them deal with the consequences too. You can't shield them from consequences all the time. Because like failure, natural consequences are another important lesson they need to learn.

Consequences allow us to face our failure head on. It allows us to know the extent of our decision and how harmful or unsafe it can be for us. The difference with natural consequences is that it isn't a sort of a punishment you set up for them but rather a natural penalty that they have to pay. It is like if you eat too much junk food, you will have digestive problems. If you watch too much TV, your head starts to ache. If you jog on a hilly trek, your legs will hurt. All these are natural consequences of the actions we choose to do. As a parent, you don't instill them in your child.

You just get out of the way and let them face the ramifications of their mistakes.

Why Natural Consequences Are Essential?

Sometimes, when parents are too overprotective of their children, they try to shield them from all natural consequences. It does say a lot about the intensity with which you love them, but this act does them more harm than good. When children remain clung to their parents, they become deprived of the opportunity to bounce back from failure. They never learn how to recover from their mistakes or learn how to regulate negative behaviors when things go wrong. Both of these skills are essential to learning, especially when they are growing up. You can't expect them to learn how to have a respectable conversation with someone if you do most of the talking for them. You can't expect them to learn to handle their fights or stand up for themselves if you keep getting involved. You can't expect them to follow the rules you have set for them if they don't know why they need to follow them, and what will happen if they don't.

They should be trained to own up to their mistakes from early on. If they act out or don't listen, let them face the consequence. If they persist on not wearing the jacket to school during a rough winter, let them manage on their own without the jacket once. Let them sense the regret when they feel like they would freeze without one. Another reason natural consequences must be enforced is that they prepare them for adulthood. When kids with ADHD experience the fruits of their actions, they are more likely to do better. It is only possible if they can link their actions with consequences.

Natural consequences also allow children with ADHD to build problem-solving skills. When they face the consequences of their actions and behaviors and don't like them, they look for ways to improve the result.

Next, it also helps parents avoid power struggles. You don't come in the way of your child and allow them to do things their way on their terms and conditions. They have no one to blame if they fail in their cause, because it was their idea. There are no arguments to be had or accusations to be made, because no one forced them to make the choice.

The reason we are stating all this is that children with ADHD need to be reminded of this from time to time. As parents, it is on us to teach them about why consequences can be bad for them and why they should try to limit negative behaviors. They should know that if they lie, people will stop trusting their word and if they speak ill of others behind their backs, no one would want to be their friend. If they create chaos everywhere they go, they will be labeled as troublesome and disobedient.

Another crucial thing you need to teach them is to be able to differentiate between positive and negative consequences. Where negative consequences are mostly reactive, positive consequences are proactive. Positive consequences encourage children to repeat good behaviors while negative consequences remind them of the behaviors they need to change. As their mentor, you have to encourage and reward positive behaviors with positive consequences like privileges, tangible prizes and gifts, and appreciation and recognition. You also have to use negative consequences sometimes like time-outs to improve behavior.

How to Discourage Bad Behavior and Mischief

When trying to limit mischief and improve negative behaviors, consequences can come in many forms. As stated above, they can be both positive and negative. But how do you use them to reinforce positive behaviors? Let's take a look!

Be Consistent

The first key thing to note is that when it comes to setting reasonable consequences, you have to ensure their enforcement. You can't just scare them off and let them get off the hook with a warning. You have to put into practice the scheduled consequences so that negative behaviors aren't repeated.

Don't Discipline in Front of Others

Sometimes, parents fail to judge their audience and start to yell or punish bad behavior right in front of others. Little do they know, children have self-esteem too. Disciplining a child with ADHD in front of a crowd can lead to poor self-esteem and low self-worth. They may start to see themselves as a failure and give up on themselves. Although it will limit bad behavior, it will also take away their confidence. Thus, this is not recommended at all.

Use Time-Ins

For many years, we have been told that to improve behavior or limit disobedience, you have to give your child a time-out where they feel the guilt and shame they have caused. However, recent studies are only proving this strategy as less effective. Time-ins, on the other hand, have been proven more effective to prevent bad behavior. Time-ins allow the child and parent to bond and reflect over the mistakes they made and talk about the consequences they may have to face. For instance, instead of telling your son to go to his room because he performed poorly on a test won't do much good as opposed to sitting him down and talking about the reasons and consequences they may have to face if they don't do well the next time.

Adjust Your Expectations

You can't change all the things that your child does. You will have to pick your battles and choose agendas worth fighting. You will have to ignore some minor issues and work on other more important things like disrespecting others, lying, or stealing.

Chapter 8: Vital Parenting Skill – Ignore Mild Misbehavior

Children with ADHD, unlike most kids, exhibit attention-seeking behavior. They want to be noticed. They want to be attended to. It doesn't matter to them if good or bad behavior gets the job done. However, when we give them attention when they do something wrong and not when they do something right, they start to assume that negative behavior is the way to go. They begin to depict more bad behavior which can make the mums and dads go mad.

Thus, this next parenting skill is more of an art where you deliberately ignore misbehavior in the hopes that they will give it up on their own.

Choosing to ignore certain behaviors doesn't mean you pay no attention to their distress or anger. If they genuinely seem in pain or emotionally-troubled, you need to be there for them. Ignoring mild misbehavior means that you ignore the way they are behaving, not how they are feeling. Attention, in itself, is a big positive reinforcement, even if it comes out of negative action. But when you choose to not give it to them purposely, they look for other ways to get it. Thus, it is important that good behavior gets attention every time it is noticeable to encourage it.

Ignoring mild misbehavior also discourages it from being repeated and prevents power struggles. Ever had a moment where your child dropped to the floor in a busy grocery store because they wanted something? Well, it is their way of getting attention. But yelling and shouting only makes it worse, doesn't it? It is because when we do that, we unknowingly give them the attention they seek. To save ourselves from further embarrassment, we let them have what they want, which in a way, reinforces that behavior. When you choose to ignore the temper tantrum and pretend that it isn't effective, they try other means to get to you. This is a silent yet a strategic way of letting them know that being obnoxious won't get them the desired results.

Why Do You Need to Keep Your Cool?

Another thing that happens frequently with many parents raising a child with ADHD is that they lose their patience after some time. They resort to yelling, shouting, and setting harsh punishments in hope that it will prevent misbehavior. Sadly, it doesn't work that way. Remaining calm and keeping your cool, on the other hand, does!

It is researchers at Ohio State University who believe so. The study offered biological evidence that positive parenting - parenting without punishments or using care and compassion to deal with misbehavior – may help children with ADHD master their behaviors and emotions (Bell et al., 2017). The study included both children with developmental disorders and their parents. Theodore Beauchaine, the leading author of the study was surprised to report that the psychological impact of praises and compliments instead of shouting and criticizing were almost instant.

The responses of the participants were monitored and evaluated during a special intervention program. The intervention program offered small group sessions for children and parents. The parents learned how to respond to their children's behaviors and the children were taught some strategies for anger management, emotion regulation, and emotionally aware and appropriate social behaviors. The researchers assigned renowned therapists to work with ninety-nine children aged four to six with ADHD. Two-thirds of the children were boys. Beauchaine believed that often these children had strained relationships with their peers, teachers, and parents. Thus, during the sessions, parents were taught better disciplining strategies. They were reminded of how they can sometimes overreact and get physical while trying to discipline their kids with ADHD. He suggested that it was common for parents to slip into negative behaviors when they felt frustrated and tired by the actions of their child.

He proposed that when parents were introduced to the concept of positive parenting, they instantly knew what it entailed. They knew that praises, smiling, flexibility, hugging, focusing on rewards and privileges, setting achievable goals and expectations can help discipline them in a less threatening and adverse way.

As weeks passed by and parents learned of effective problem-solving techniques, positive parenting responses, and adaptive emotional regulation, the children also began to depict improvement in their behavior. Additionally, following the intervention, it was also notable that the heart rates of the children with ADHD slowed down a little and their breathing became calmer. All of this happened in just two months when the researchers predicted that the behavioral changes will start to show well after one year. To further prove that the behavioral improvements were the result of the intervention program, he divided families into two groups. One group received 20 weeks' worth of sessions whereas the other received only 10 sessions. The behavioral changes in the first group were more evident and long-lasting than the ones depicted by the children of parents in the second group. In his concluding remarks, Beauchaine proposed that the earlier parents of children with ADHD started taking therapy and practicing positive parenting, the better the results will be.

How to Improve Misbehavior Without Yelling or Shouting

Parenting kids with ADHD is a challenge for many parents. It is a test of their patience and good judgment to the point where they end up making bad decisions while disciplining misbehavior. Yelling and shouting don't always work but choosing compassionate approaches surely does. Below are some friendly approaches to discipline misbehavior without losing your mind.

Keep it Short

When disciplining your child, be concise. Many parenting experts believe that the best way to discipline children with ADHD is to use fewer words. The more direct you are with your commands and orders, the more effective they will be. Be very clear about what is expected of them so that they can hear and remember it.

Don't Bully Into Submission

When we yell at our kids, we generate fear. This is no less than a form of bullying where they begin to behave out of fear not out of their own will. Thus, you have to show them that you care and look them in the eye when telling them how valuable they are and how grateful and proud you will be when they behave well. You can achieve a lot more when you talk to them, not at them.

Choose an Appropriate Time to Have a Talk

Every child wants to feel valued and respected. They want to feel validated and important. Thus, when they do something you don't like or agree with, ignore it instead of yelling at them at the moment. Choose another time to bring it up and talk about it in a calm and composed manner.

Be Proactive When Discussing Negative Consequences

Another great approach to handle misbehavior is to make them aware of the consequences that await them if they break the rules. When setting consequences, you can use strategies like time-outs or taking away privileges to discipline them and learn from their mistakes. If any other consequences put them off, communicate them beforehand to prevent misbehavior before it even begins.

Set Punishments for Misbehavior

Appropriate punishments are another approachable way as long as they aren't too harsh or demeaning. For instance, suppose the child has spilled some juice on the kitchen tiles. An appropriate punishment would be to ask them to clean the mess instead of belittling them for their poor handling of the glass and being hyperactive.

Chapter 9: Vital Parenting Skill – Give Positive Attention

Parenting a child with attention or hyperactivity disorder can be both challenging and exhausting. The children are always brimming with energy and want to be attended constantly. This can tire out even the most patient and tolerating parent. But in recent times, positive attention is considered one of the greatest parenting skills and thought of as a good investment.

But what does it mean to give your child positive attention?

The core idea behind positive attention is to praise positive behaviors and actions instead of reacting to negative behaviors. It is very common for parents to get annoyed, and sometimes lose their patience when their child does something they aren't supposed to. However, when the same child does something good and expects praise, parents often fall short. After all, why should they be rewarded for something they are supposed to do? Positive attention requires a change in approach to the way we interact with our children. It teaches us not only to be patient and kind but also to ignore behaviors that are not-so-good and praise the ones that are.

Positive attention can be further explained in several forms. It can come in the form of a hug, a pat on the back, smile, compassion, and empathy and praises, and recognition. It can also come in the form of quality time spent with the child where they feel like they are the center of attention and feel validated.

Positive Attention and Its Benefits for Children With ADHD

Having a positive and healthy relationship with your child is important for many reasons – discipline being one of them. When a healthy relationship is established between you and the child, they strive to do better under your mentorship.

Would you not be more motivated to work under someone that respects you and shows you appreciation too? Or would you be okay working under someone that never appreciates you or shows you any respect?

Parents who spend quality time with their children and offer praise and appreciation wholeheartedly raise compassionate and confident children. When children with ADHD feel respected and encouraged to do better, it serves as a motivating factor. Daily doses of affection and positive praise can reduce behavioral problems. It can also strengthen the bond between you and your child. Moreover, they will stop trying to seek attention by acting out, crying, or shouting. They will also avoid repeating the same mistakes over and over again. They will also keep to themselves and not poke their noses in others matters.

Tips for Daily Doses of Positive Attention

When quality time is valued and efforts are made to make communication more prevalent, the child also starts to look forward to spending time with you. This is especially important if your child is already a teenager and started to spend more time in their room, immersed in their phones than with you or their siblings. Additionally, they will be more driven to follow the rules and expectations as well as listen to what you have to say. So how can we encourage communication with daily doses of positive attention? Let's take a look!

Be Positive With Your Praise

There are times when you unintentionally call out bad behavior in a demeaning and insulting tone. It just happens out of habit. When dealing with children with ADHD, we have to improve on the way we comment on behaviors – both positive and negative. As we now know that the very goal of positive attention is to praise positivity and ignore negativity, the first thing you need to do is mold your sentences in a way that they come off as positive, even when trying to prevent misbehavior. For example, instead of saying, "Why did you bring your dirty shoes inside," say something like, "Oh, I see you have mistakenly brought your shoes inside with you" – the same thing but in a positive manner.

Resist the Urge to Correct

Again, as parents, we want to save our children from harm and pain. So we are quick to spot something wrong and try to correct them. Don't do that. Encourage them to imagine things differently. If they want to paint an apple purple, let them. If they want to give cows a pair of wings, hell yes! It will make them feel more confident in their abilities and you can always choose another time to correct them subtly.

Abolish Distractions When Interacting

When spending time with them and appreciating their efforts, do it whole-heartedly while being present in the moment. This means that you have to put down your phones, switch off the TV, and listen to them. Distractions can undermine their self-worth. They may not feel as important and validated when they feel you aren't 100% interested in what they have to say or do. Besides, distractions will also prevent them from completing things.

Give Them Undivided Attention Daily

Ideally, you should give them at least 15 to 20 minutes of undivided attention every day. You can do things together and sit down with them in their free time and have a real one-on-one conversation about their school, peers, and aspirations. It's simple math. When you listen to them, they will listen to you.

Make Interactions More Meaningful

This means choosing activities they are interested in. You must introduce to them games and activities that boost their attention and require them to stay focused. If confused, let them pick what they want to do for the time being and just get along with them.

Conclusion

Raising a child with ADHD can be mentally-draining. They need more attention, extra time, and extreme patience. Indeed, they aren't deliberately trying to be difficult but it makes it difficult for parents to deal with them, especially when they have little knowledge of how to.

Hopefully, this book will be a good start to learn of some great parenting skills in case your child has been recently diagnosed with the disorder. However, there is one thing that it didn't cover. The one thing that, perhaps, is the most important of all: Self-care!

No one can prepare you for the battle you are heading into but you can't win unless you are prepared for it. You have to take care of yourself first to be able to take care of your child. Chances are, they are going to be needing every last bit of energy. This requires that you are mentally and physically prepared for it. You have to get rid of all the negative self-talk about how it must have been your fault. You also have to stop worrying about how you are going to raise them or whether or not you are able to do enough.

Next comes, taking care of your health and wellbeing. You will need to find ways to manage your stress and anger. You will have to learn ways to identify the triggers that build frustration and find healthy ways to vent it out. A big part of this starts with the right diet and foods that alleviate stress levels and release happiness-inducing chemicals.

Remember, you are your child's first role model. You need to lead by example. If you take care of yourself, they will learn to take care of themselves too. If you cope with stress and impatience in healthy ways, they will do the same. On the other hand, if they always find you running out of patience or overtired, you will be setting the wrong example to follow and risk losing sight of support and structure you want them to have in their lives.

So treat yourself well first, and then tend to your child with ADHD.

Thank you for giving this a read. I hope you loved it too because I certainly enjoyed writing it. It would make me the happiest if you would take a moment to leave an honest review. All you have to do is visit the site from where you purchased it. It's that simple! It doesn't have to be a full-fledged paragraph, just a few words will do too. Your few words will help others decide if this is what they should be reading too. Thank you in advance and best of luck with your parenting excursions. Surely, every moment is a joyous one with a kid.

References

Attention-Deficit/Hyperactivity Disorder (ADHD).
(2017). Cleveland Clinic.
https://my.clevelandclinic.org/health/diseas
es/4784-attention-deficithyperactivity-
disorder-adhd

Bell, Z., Shader, T., Webster-Stratton, C., Reid, M. J.,
& Beauchaine, T. P. (2017). Improvements in
Negative Parenting Mediate Changes in
Children's Autonomic Responding Following
a Preschool Intervention for ADHD. Clinical
Psychological Science, 6(1), 134–144.
https://doi.org/10.1177/2167702617727559

Celebrity Spotlight: How Michael Phelps' ADHD
Helped Him Make Olympic History. (n.d.).
Understood.
https://www.understood.org/en/learning-
thinking-differences/personal-
stories/famous-people/celebrity-spotlight-
how-michael-phelps-adhd-helped-him-make-
olympic-history

Common Challenges of Parenting a Child With
ADHD, Dyslexia or Learning Differences.
(n.d.). Brain Balance. Retrieved June 8, 2020,
from
https://blog.brainbalancecenters.com/2015/1
0/common-challenges-of-parenting-a-child-
with-adhd-dyslexia-or-learning-differences

Flippin, R. (2007, October 6). Hyperfocus: The
    ADHD Phenomenon of Intense Fixation.
    ADDitude.
    https://www.additudemag.com/understandi
    ng-adhd-hyperfocus/

Groom, M. J., Scerif, G., Liddle, P. F., Batty, M. J.,
    Liddle, E. B., Roberts, K. L., Cahill, J. D.,
    Liotti, M., & Hollis, C. (2009). Effects of
    Motivation and Medication on
    Electrophysiological Markers of Response
    Inhibition in Children with Attention-
    Deficit/Hyperactivity Disorder. Biological
    Psychiatry, 67(7), 624–631.
    https://doi.org/10.1016/j.biopsych.2009.09.
    029

LaMagna, M. (2018, May 6). Richard Branson says
    this one thing helped him become a better
    entrepreneur.   MarketWatch.
    https://www.marketwatch.com/story/overco
    ming-childhood-taunts-richard-branson-
    says-this-early-challenge-helped-him-
    succeed-in-business-2018-05-04

Law, E. C., Sideridis, G. D., Prock, L. A., & Sheridan,
    M. A. (2014). Attention-Deficit/Hyperactivity
    Disorder in Young Children: Predictors of
    Diagnostic Stability. PEDIATRICS, 133(4),
    659–667.
    https://doi.org/10.1542/peds.2013-3433

Low, K. (2019a, June 17). How Parents Can Make an Easier Life for Their Child With ADHD. Verywell Mind. https://www.verywellmind.com/understanding-children-with-adhd-20686

Low, K. (2019b, August 13). Children With ADHD Need Structure in Their Lives to Stay Focused. Verywell Mind. https://www.verywellmind.com/why-is-structure-important-for-kids-with-adhd-20747#:~:text=The%20symptoms%20of%20ADHD%20lead

Low, K. (2020, January 7). How to Set up a Reward System for Improving Your Child's ADHD Behavior. Verywell Mind. https://www.verywellmind.com/behavior-management-for-adhd-20867

Miller, G. (2017, November 16). Calm Parents Help Calm Kids With ADHD. WebMD. https://www.webmd.com/add-adhd/news/20171116/calm-parents-help-calm-kids-with-adhd#1

Morin, A. (2019a, February 13). How to Create a Token Economy System That Will Motivate Your Child. Verywell Family. https://www.verywellfamily.com/create-a-token-economy-system-to-improve-child-behavior-1094888

Morin, A. (2019b, June 24). Why Ignoring Is the Best Way to Deal With Certain Behavior Problems. Verywell Family. https://www.verywellfamily.com/is-it-really-ok-to-ignore-mild-misbehaviors-1094791#:~:text=When%20you%20ignore%20your%20child

Morin, A. (2019c, September 12). How to Make Natural Consequences an Effective Discipline Tool. Verywell Family. https://www.verywellfamily.com/natural-consequences-as-a-discipline-strategy-1094849

Sturiale, J. (2015, October 14). Stop Yelling At Your Kids. WebMD. https://www.webmd.com/parenting/features/stop-yelling-at-your-kids#1

Understanding ADHD: Information for Parents. (2019, September 25). HealthyChildren.Org. https://www.healthychildren.org/English/health-issues/conditions/adhd/Pages/Understanding-ADHD.aspx

Vann, M. R. (2013, September 19). Create a Daily Routine for Children With ADHD | Everyday Health. Everyday Health. https://www.everydayhealth.com/add-adhd/create-a-daily-routine-for-children-with-adhd.aspx

Wymbs, B. T., Pelham, W. E., Molina, B. S. G.,
Gnagy, E. M., Wilson, T. K., & Greenhouse, J.
B. (2008). Rate and predictors of divorce
among parents of youths with ADHD. Journal
of Consulting and Clinical Psychology, 76(5),
735–744. https://doi.org/10.1037/a0012719

Made in the USA
Coppell, TX
17 January 2023